CLIP ART OF THE OLD TESTAMENT

De La Salle House

CLIP ART
OF THE OLD TESTAMENT

Artwork by
Helen Siegl

A PUEBLO BOOK

The Liturgical Press   Collegeville, Minnesota

A Pueblo Book published by The Liturgical Press.

Cover design by Ann Blattner.

ISBN 0-8146-6010-X

CONTENTS

THE BOOK OF GENESIS

1:1-2   *In the beginning of creation when God made heaven and earth the earth was without form and void,* **3**

1:6-8   *The Second Day,* **3**

1:9-13   *The Third Day,* **3**

1:14-19   *The Fourth Day,* **5**

1:20-23   *The Fifth Day,* **5**

1:24-31   *The Sixth Day,* **5**

2   *Garden of Eden,* **7**

3   *The expulsion from Paradise,* **7**

4:8   *Cain attacked his brother Abel,* **9**

7   *Noah building the ark,* **11**

7   *Noah and the ark,* **13**

11   *The Tower of Babel,* **13**

14:18   *Then Melchizedek, king of Salem, brought food and wine. He was priest of God most high, and he pronounced his blessing on Abram,* **15**

15:5   *Look up into the sky and count the stars if you can. So many shall your descendants be,* **15**

18:12   *Sarah laughed to herself and said, ''I am past bearing children now that I am out of my time and my husband is old,''* **15**

18:32   *O Lord, if I speak just once more—suppose ten could be found there? He said, ''For the sake of the ten, I will not destroy it,''* **17**

19:26   *Lot's wife looked back and she turned into a pillar of salt,* **17**

22:10   *Abraham sacrificing Isaac,* **17**

24:17-19   *Abraham's servant said to her: ''Give me a sip of water from your jar.'' Rebecca answered: ''Drink, sir, . . . and I shall water your camels also,''* **19**

27:25   *Isaac blessing Jacob,* **19**

28   *Jacob's dream,* **21**

29:10   *Jacob saw Rachel, the daughter of Laban, his mother's brother, with Laban's flock. He rolled the stone off the mouth of the well and watered Laban's sheep,* **23**

32:25   *Jacob wrestling with the angel,* **23**

37   *Joseph's dream,* **25**

45:4   *I am your brother Joseph, whom you sold into Egypt,* **25**

47   *Jacob before the Pharaoh,* **25**

THE BOOK OF EXODUS

2	*Moses in the bull rushes,* **27**	
3:3	*Moses and the burning bush,* **27**	
7–11	*Ten Plagues,* **29**	
12	*The Passover,* **31**	
13:21	*The Lord went before them, by day a pillar of cloud, by night a pillar of fire,* **31**	
14:21	*Moses stretched out his hand over the sea,* **33**	
15:20	*Miriam dancing,* **33**	
16:4	*I will rain down bread from heaven for you,* **35**	
17:6	*Strike the rock,* **35**	
17:12	*Aaron and Hur held up his hands,* **37**	
24	*Moses wrote down all the words of the Lord,* **37**	
24	*So Moses went up the mountain and a cloud covered the mountain for six days,* **39**	
32:8	*These are your gods, Israel,* **41**	
32:8	*They have made themselves an image of a bull-calf, they have prostrated themselves before it, sacrificed to it and said, ''These are your gods, O Israel, that brought you up from Egypt,''* **41**	

THE BOOK OF NUMBERS

10:1-2	*The Lord spoke to Moses, ''Make two trumpets of silver,''* **43**
13:23	*They cut a branch with a single bunch of grapes,* **43**

THE BOOK OF DEUTERONOMY

6:4, 6	*Hear, O Israel, the Lord is our God. These Commandments which I give you this day are to be kept in your heart,* **45**
34	*The death of Moses,* **45**

THE BOOK OF JOSHUA

4:8	*They lifted up 12 stones from the middle of the Jordan,* **47**
7:25	*The stoning of Achan,* **47**

THE BOOK OF JUDGES

4:4	*Deborah, a prophetess, was judge in Israel,* **49**
7:5	*Every man who laps the water like a dog stand on one side and on the other every man who goes down on his knees and drinks,* **49**

THE BOOK OF RUTH

1:16	*Where you go, I will go, and where you stay, I will stay. Your people shall be my people, and your God my God,* **51**

THE FIRST BOOK OF SAMUEL

2:1   *Then Hannah offered this prayer: "My heart rejoices in the Lord, in the Lord I now hold my head high. My mouth is full of derision of my foes, exultant because thou hast saved me,"* **53**

26:12 *David took the spear and the water jar from beside Saul's head,* **53**

THE SECOND BOOK OF SAMUEL

5:3   *They anointed David king over Israel,* **55**

7:2   *Here I live in a house of cedar, while the ark of God is housed in curtains,* **55**

THE FIRST BOOK OF KINGS

8:22-23 *Solomon spread out his hands toward heaven and said: "O Lord God of Israel, there is no God like thee in heaven above or on earth beneath,"* **57**

11   *Go and stand on the mount before the Lord,* **57**

19:5   *He lay down under the bush and, while he slept, an angel touched him and said, "Rise and eat,"* **57**

THE SECOND BOOK OF KINGS

4   *The Shunammite woman,* **59**

4:36   *"Call this Shunammite woman," Elisha said. She answered his call and the prophet said, "Take your child,"* **59**

THE BOOK OF NEHEMIAH

8:2   *Ezra the priest brought the law before the assembly,* **61**

THE BOOK OF TOBIT

11:4   *Raphael said to Tobias, "Take the fish-gall in your hand." The dog went with the angel and Tobias, following at their heels,* **63**

THE BOOK OF ESTHER

5:3   *What is it, Queen Esther? Whatever you ask of me up to half my kingdom shall be given to you,* **65**

THE BOOK OF JOB

2:7-8 *Satan smote Job with running sores from head to foot, so that he took a piece of broken pot to scratch himself as he sat among ashes,* **67**

2:13   *For seven days and seven nights they sat beside him on the ground and none of them said a word to him,* **67**

THE BOOK OF PROVERBS

8:22, 31 *The Lord created me in the beginning of his works before all else that he made long ago . . . playing on the earth, when he had finished it, while my delight was in mankind,* **69**

9:1-2   *Wisdom has built her house. She has hewn her 7 pillars. She has killed a beast, spiced her wine, and she has spread her table,* **69**

THE SONG OF SONGS
3:1-2   *I have sought my true love, I said, "I will rise and go the rounds of the city, through the streets and the squares seeking my true love,"* **71**

THE BOOK OF WISDOM
7:8, 10   *I valued her above scepters and thrones. I loved her more than health and beauty,* **73**

11:21-22   *Great strength is thine to exert at any moment, and the power of thy arm no man can resist, for in thy sight the whole world is like a grain,* **73**

THE BOOK OF SIRACH
3:12   *O child, help your father in his old age,* **75**

27:6-7   *As the fruit of the tree reveals the skill of the grower, so the expression of a man's thought reveals his character. Do not praise a man till you hear him in discussion, for this is the test,* **75**

35:14   *He never ignores the appeal of the orphan or the widow when she pours out her complaint,* **75**

THE BOOK OF SIRACH (ECCLESIASTICUS)
3:30   *An attentive ear is the desire of the wise. As water quenches a blazing fire, so almsgiving atones for sin,* **77**

THE BOOK OF ISAIAH
6-8   *I heard the voice of the Lord saying, "Whom shall I send? Who will go for me?" And I answered, "Here I am, send me,"* **79**

9:1   *The people who walked in darkness have seen a great light,* **79**

11:6   *The wolf shall live with the sheep,* **79**

35:5-6   *The eyes of the blind shall be opened and the ears of the deaf unstopped. Then shall the lame man leap like a deer,* **81**

40:3   *Prepare a road for the Lord through the wilderness,* **81**

40:11   *He will carry the lambs in his bosom and lead the ewes to water,* **83**

43:20   *The wild beast shall do me honor, the wolf and the ostrich, for I will provide water in the wilderness and rivers in the barren desert,* **83**

49:15   *Can a woman forget the infant at her breast or a loving mother the child of her womb?* **85**

50:6   *I offered my back to the lash and let my beard be plucked from my chin,* **85**

52   *Suffering servants,* **85**

52:1-2   *Awake, awake, put on your strength, O Zion; put on your loveliest garments, holy city of Jerusalem, O captive daughter of Zion,* **87**

55:1   *Come, all who are thirsty, come, fetch water,* **87**

58:7   *Is it not sharing your food with the hungry, clothing the naked when you meet them?* **89**

58:7   *Is not sharing your food with the hungry, taking the homeless poor into your house, clothing the naked when you meet them, and never evading a duty to your kinsfolk?* **89**

60   *A multitude of camels shall cover you,* **91**

61:3   *To give them garlands instead of ashes, oil of gladness instead of mourner's tears,* **91**

62:4   *For the Lord delights in you and to him your land is wedded,* **91**

THE BOOK OF JEREMIAH

1:9-10   *The Lord stretched out his hand and touched my mouth and said to me: "I put my words into your mouth. This day I give you authority over nations,"* **93**

17:7-8   *Blessed the man who trusts in the Lord, he shall be like a tree planted by the waterside,* **93**

20:7   *O Lord, you have deceived me and I was deceived,* **93**

31:7   *Break into shouts of joy for Jacob's sake, lead the nations, crying loud and clear, singing out your praises. Say the Lord has saved his people,* **95**

38:6   *They took Jeremiah and threw him into the pit. There was no water in the pit, only mud, and Jeremiah sank in the mud,* **95**

THE BOOK OF EZEKIEL

17:22-23   *I will take a slip from the lofty crown of the cedar, I will plant it high on a lofty mountain,* **97**

34:11   *I myself will ask after my sheep and go in search of them,* **97**

37:4   *O dry bones, hear the word of the Lord,* **97**

THE BOOK OF DANIEL

3   *Blessed is the God of Shadrach, Meshach, and Abednego,* **99**

6:21   *Daniel, servant of the living God, has your God whom you serve continually been able to save you from the lions?* **101**

7:14   *Sovereignty and glory and kingly power were given to him, so that all people and nations of every language should serve him,* **103**

12:1   *At that moment Michael shall appear, Michael the great captain who stands guard over your fellow countrymen,* **103**

THE BOOK OF AMOS

7:8   *I am setting a plumb line to the heart of my people Israel,* **105**

THE BOOK OF JONAH

1:15; 2:1   *They took Jonah and threw him overboard and the sea stopped raging. . . . The Lord ordained that a great fish should swallow Jonah, and for 3 days and 3 nights he remained in his belly,* **107**

3:4-5   *Jonah proclaimed, "In forty days Nineveh shall be overthrown." The people of Nineveh believed God's word. They ordered a public fast and put on sackcloth,* **107**

THE BOOK OF MICAH

THE BOOK OF ZEPHANIAH

WOMEN OF THE OLD TESTAMENT

MISCELLANEOUS,

THE OLD TESTAMENT

THE BOOK OF GENESIS

IN THE BEGINNING OF CREATION WHEN GOD MADE HEAVEN & EARTH THE EARTH WAS WITHOUT FORM AND VOID

Genesis 1:1-2

THE SECOND DAY

Genesis 1:6-8

THE THIRD DAY

Genesis 1:9-13

THE BOOK OF GENESIS

Genesis 1:14-19

Genesis 1:20-23

Genesis 1:24-31

THE BOOK OF GENESIS

Genesis 2

Genesis 3

Genesis 4:8

Genesis 7

THE BOOK OF GENESIS

Genesis 7

Genesis 11

THE BOOK OF GENESIS

Genesis 14:18

Genesis 15:5

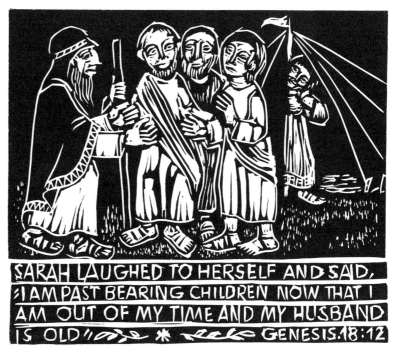

Genesis 18:12

Genesis 18:32

Genesis 19:26

Genesis 22:10

THE BOOK OF GENESIS

ABRAHAM'S SERVANT SAID TO HER: "GIVE ME A SIP OF WATER FROM YOUR JAR." REBECCA ANSWERED: "DRINK, SIR, AND I SHALL WATER YOUR CAMELS ALSO." — GENESIS·24:17-19

Genesis 24:17–19

ISAAC BLESSING JACOB·GENESIS·27:25

Genesis 27:25

Genesis 28

Genesis 29:10

Genesis 32:25

THE BOOK OF GENESIS

Genesis 37

Genesis 45:4

Genesis 47

THE BOOK OF EXODUS

Exodus 2

Exodus 3:3

Exodus 7–11

THE BOOK OF EXODUS

Exodus 12

Exodus 13:21

THE BOOK OF EXODUS

Exodus 14:21

Exodus 15:20

Exodus 16:4

Exodus 17:6

Exodus 17:12

Exodus 24

Exodus 24

Exodus 32:8

Exodus 32:8

THE BOOK OF NUMBERS

Numbers 10:1-2

Numbers 13:23

THE BOOK OF DEUTERONOMY

Deuteronomy 6:4, 6

Deuteronomy 34

THE BOOK OF JOSHUA

Joshua 4:8

Joshua 7:25

THE BOOK OF JUDGES

Judges 4:4

Judges 7:5

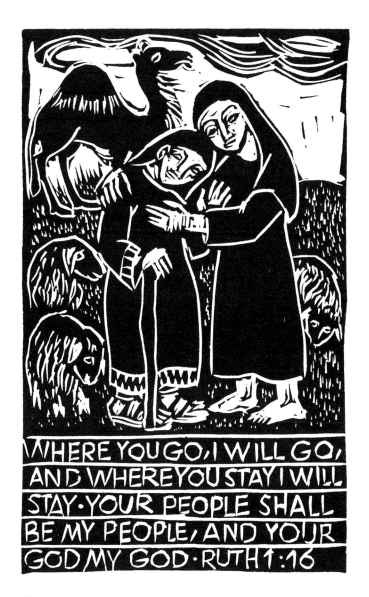

Ruth 1:16

1 Samuel 2:1

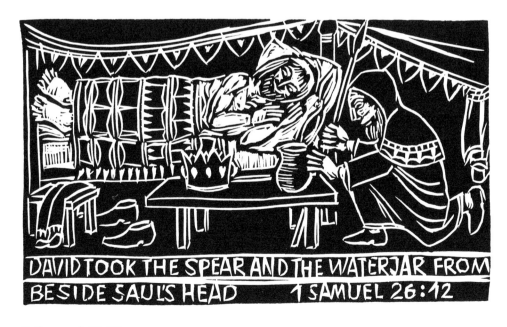

1 Samuel 26:12

THE SECOND BOOK OF SAMUEL

2 Samuel 5:3

2 Samuel 7:2

THE FIRST BOOK OF KINGS

1 Kings 8:22-23

1 Kings 11

1 Kings 19:5

THE SECOND BOOK OF KINGS

2 Kings 4

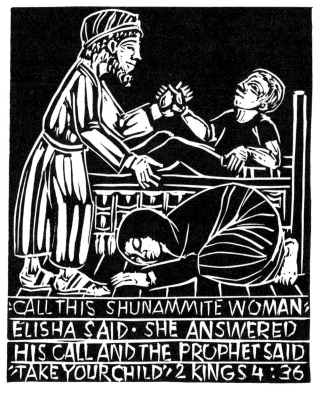

2 Kings 4:36

Nehemiah 8:2

RAPHAEL SAID TO TOBIAS "TAKE THE FISH-GALL IN YOUR HAND" THE DOG WENT WITH THE ANGEL AND TOBIAS, FOLLOWING AT THEIR HEELS · TOBIT 11:4

Tobit 11:4

Esther 5:3

Job 2:7-8

Job 2:13

THE BOOK OF PROVERBS

Proverbs 8:22, 31

Proverbs 9:1-2

Song of Songs 3:1-2

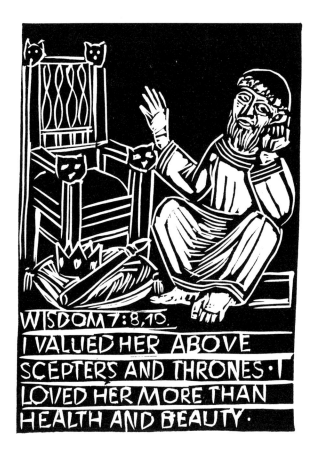

Wisdom 7:8, 10

Wisdom 11:21-22

THE BOOK OF SIRACH

Sirach 3:12

Sirach 27:6-7

Sirach 35:14

THE BOOK OF SIRACH (ECCLESIASTICUS)

Sirach (Ecclesiasticus) 3:30

Isaiah 6–8

Isaiah 9:1

Isaiah 11:6

Isaiah 35:5-6

Isaiah 40:3

Isaiah 40:11

Isaiah 43:20

Isaiah 49:15

Isaiah 50:6

Isaiah 52

Isaiah 52:1-2

Isaiah 55:1

Isaiah 58:7

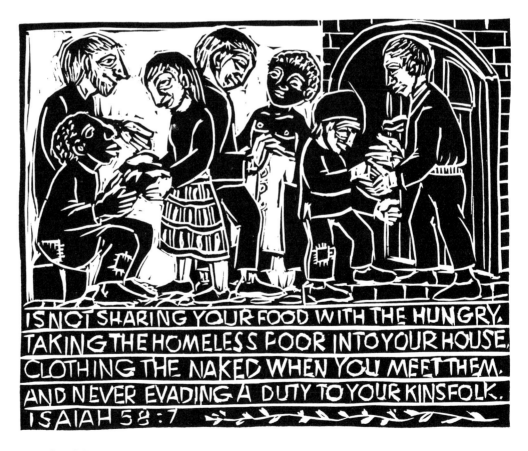

Isaiah 58:7

THE BOOK OF ISAIAH

Isaiah 60

Isaiah 61:3

Isaiah 62:4

THE BOOK OF JEREMIAH

Jeremiah 1:9-10

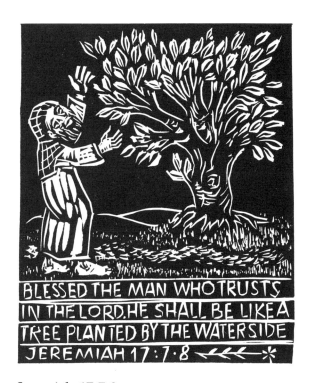

Jeremiah 17:7-8

Jeremiah 20:7

Jeremiah 31:7

Jeremiah 38:6

Ezekiel 17:22-23

Ezekiel 34:11

Ezekiel 37:4

Daniel 3

Daniel 6:21

Daniel 7:14

Daniel 12:1

Amos 7:8

THE BOOK OF JONAH

Jonah 1:15; 2:1

Jonah 3:4-5

Micah 5:3

Zephaniah 3

Zephaniah 3:14

WOMEN OF THE OLD TESTAMENT

Ruth and Naomi

Hannah

Rebekah

Miriam

MISCELLANEOUS

MISCELLANEOUS